A Million Llamas

Michael O'Mara Books Limited

T0383497

First published in Great Britain in 2021 by Michael O'Mara Books Limited,
9 Lion Yard, Tremadoc Road, London SW4 7NQ

 www.mombooks.com

Michael O'Mara Books

@OMaraBooks

@OMaraBooks

Copyright © Lulu Mayo 2021

All rights reserved. No part of this book may be reproduced, stored in a retrieval system, or
transmitted in any form or by any means, without the prior permission in writing of the publisher, nor
be otherwise circulated in any form of binding or cover other than that in which it is published and
without a similar condition including this condition being imposed on the subsequent purchaser.

A CIP catalogue record for this book is available from the British Library.

ISBN: 978-1-78929-270-1

3 5 7 9 10 8 6 4 2

This book was printed in China.

Illustrated by

Lulu Mayo